explaining...

CYSTIC FIBROSIS

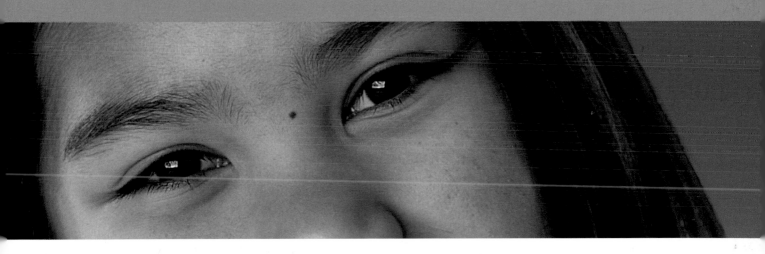

W

FRANKLIN WATTS
LONDON • SYDNEY

IAN POWELL

First published in 2009 by
Franklin Watts
338 Euston Road
London NW1 3BH

Franklin Watts Australia
Level 17/207 Kent Street
Sydney NSW 2000

© 2009 Franklin Watts

ISBN 978 0 7496 8257 6

Dewey classification number: 362.19637

A CIP catalogue record for this publication is available from the British Library.

Planning and production by Discovery Books Limited
Managing Editor: Laura Durman
Editor: Annabel Savery
Designer: Keith Williams
Picture research: Rachel Tisdale
Consultant: Jacqui Cowlard, Cystic Fibrosis Clinical
   Nurse Specialist, Barts and The London Hospital.

Printed in China

Franklin Watts is a division of Hachette Children's Books, an Hachette Livre Company.
www.hachettelivre.co.uk

Photo acknowledgements: Corbis: pp. 30 (Karen Kasmauski), 32 (Adriane Mol/Zefa), 38 (Rick Friedman); Getty Images: pp. 21 (Science Faction), 39 (M J Kim); www.JohnBirdsall.co.uk: pp. 15, 33; Istockphoto.com: cover top (Jani Bryson), cover bottom right (Andrea Gingerich); pp. 12 (iofoto), 14 (Lee Pettet), 18 (Cat London), 20 (Lee Pettet), 23 (Oleg Prikhodko), 24 (Andy Green), 28 (Jared Cassidy), 29 (Amy Myers), 34 (Chris Schmidt); Library of Congress: p. 11; Science Photo Library: pp. 9 both (J. C. Revy), 22 (Alix), cover bottom left & 26 (Mauro Fermariello); Shutterstock: pp. 8 (Mandy Godbehear), 35 (Carsten Medom Madsen); Joe Styler: p. 37; U.S. Air Force: p. 19

Source credits: We would like to thank the following for their contribution:
Teeside Evening Gazette, January 2008.

Please note the case studies in this book are either true life stories or based on true life stories.

The pictures in the book feature a mixture of adults and children with and without cystic fibrosis. Some of the photographs feature models, and it should not be implied that they have cystic fibrosis.

Contents

What is cystic fibrosis?

Cystic fibrosis is an inherited disease, which means that children are born with it. The term 'cystic fibrosis' is often shortened to CF. Both boys and girls can be affected, but CF cannot be 'caught' or passed from one child to another.

Statistics

In the UK, five babies are born each week with cystic fibrosis, making it the most common life-threatening inherited disease. It affects around 8,000 people in the UK and around 30,000 in the United States. Although it is less common among African and some Asian races, CF is found all over the world. Although there is no cure for cystic fibrosis to date, there have been important advances in diagnosis and treatment.

▼ *Many young people with cystic fibrosis are able to live full and active lives.*

Problems

Cystic fibrosis can affect many organs in the body, especially the lungs, pancreas, liver and intestines. Normally, the lungs have a thin coating of mucus which helps them to keep out germs, but in people with cystic fibrosis, the mucus is thick and sticky. It can clog the lungs and block airways, making breathing difficult. It also makes it easier for germs to develop into infections and to cause inflammation. The thick, sticky mucus can affect the pancreas and digestive system, too. As a result, food is not properly digested, causing bowel problems and affecting energy levels and growth. People with cystic fibrosis are affected differently; some have more problems with the lungs, others with the digestive system.

Symptoms

The symptoms of cystic fibrosis can include coughing and wheezing, shortness of breath, frequent chest infections, problems absorbing food, bowel problems and poor growth and weight gain. Fifty years ago, few children with cystic fibrosis lived beyond their first year. Today, advances in treatment have improved their quality of life and the average life expectancy is now about 40.

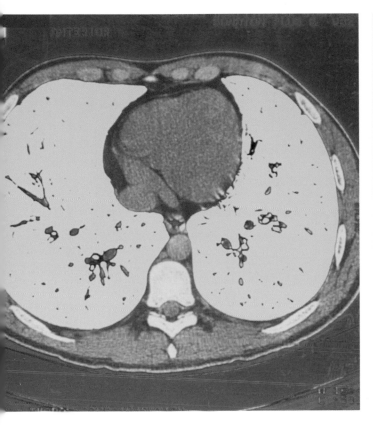 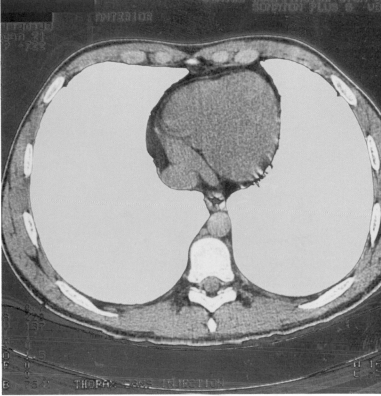

▲ *Scans of lungs of a person with CF (left) and those of a person without CF (right). The red patches indicate mucus blocking the airways in the lungs.*

Children with cystic fibrosis have to take special care of themselves, but they can lead full and active lives, enjoying friendships, school and sports.

'The outlook is a pretty positive one in terms of treatment which allows children [with cystic fibrosis] to live a relatively healthy and active lifestyle. It is a pretty rigorous heavy duty regime of medication, physiotherapy and regular hospital trips. But within that children can enjoy a relatively happy lifestyle.'
Ed Owen of the Cystic Fibrosis Trust

'SIXTY-FIVE ROSES'

'I can remember being told I had cystic fibrosis when I was quite small. At first, I quite liked all the attention, and having all these colourful tablets to take every day. I don't think I really knew what it meant for me until I was older. In our family we always called it "sixty five roses". They told me the name came from a little boy who overheard his mother talking about cystic fibrosis on the phone and thought she was saying sixty-five roses. Cystic fibrosis is quite hard to say when you are only little!'

Robert, aged 11

Cystic fibrosis: a brief history

The symptoms of cystic fibrosis have been recorded since the 1600s. In old European folklore, there are stories of mothers licking the foreheads of their children to see if they tasted salty as this is one of the symptoms of cystic fibrosis.

Dr Dorothy Andersen

By the early twentieth century, scientific studies had identified other symptoms of cystic fibrosis, such as blockages in the intestines of newborn babies. The disease was first described as 'cystic fibrosis of the pancreas' by Dr Dorothy Andersen in 1938. 'Fibrosis' means 'scarring of tissue' and 'cystic' refers to the ducts, or channels, in the body that are affected. Dr Andersen studied infant deaths at a hospital in New York. She reported a range of symptoms including blockages in the intestine, breathing problems and damage to the pancreas. She suggested that the disease might be inherited, and began using pancreatic enzymes to treat children.

Studies of cystic fibrosis symptoms continued through the 1930s and 1940s. Doctors recognised that thick mucus affected both the breathing and digestive systems. At that time, cystic fibrosis was a disease that usually led to early death in childhood from breathing problems or poor nutrition and growth.

The cystic fibrosis gene

Scientists started looking for a genetic cause for the disease from the 1940s onwards. The breakthrough came in 1989, when they isolated

THE SWEAT TEST

When it was first recognised as a disorder, the only way to diagnose cystic fibrosis was to extract pancreatic fluids to check for the telltale low levels of chemicals called enzymes in the body. A new method of diagnosis was discovered in the early 1950s by American paediatrician Paul di Sant'Agnese. He observed that infants with CF who collapsed during the New York heat waves of the late 1940s and early 1950s had too much salt in their sweat. This led to a simple sweat test, which proved to be a safer, easier and more accurate way of diagnosing the disease, as cystic fibrosis is detected by raised levels of salt in the sweat. Today the sweat test is still commonly used to confirm the diagnosis of CF.

▲ *Dr Dorothy Andersen (centre) was a pioneer in the diagnosis and treatment of cystic fibrosis.*

a gene which made a protein that affected the movement of salt (sodium chloride) in the body. They found that in people with cystic fibrosis, this gene, known as the CF gene, was faulty (see pages 12-13).

Although scientists are still seeking a cure, they have made great progress in understanding and treating the disease. Management of lung and digestive problems, and antibiotic treatments for lung infections have improved the lives of people with cystic fibrosis and helped them to live on into their thirties and forties.

WORKING FOR A CURE

Karen Aronowicz is a volunteer helper for the Canadian Cystic Fibrosis Foundation and mother to 11-year-old Amanda who has cystic fibrosis. She says:

'Cystic fibrosis volunteers are motivated because we are all working for that cure. The knowledge and support from the foundation has only helped me to keep going, and going with a smile on my face because I truly believe we will find a cure or effective control.'

What causes cystic fibrosis?

Cystic fibrosis is a genetic disorder. We all inherit two copies of each of our genes, one from each parent. A gene is a set of instructions for making a chemical. Each of these chemicals has a different function in our body.

The CF gene

Your body is made up of trillions of cells. The CF gene produces a protein called the cystic fibrosis transmembrane regulator, or CFTR. This protein controls the amount of fluid lining the walls of the airways and other organs. The CFTR affects how salt and water enter and exit cells in the body. In a person with cystic fibrosis, the gene fails to produce the protein, or produces a faulty protein that blocks the transport of salt and water. As a result, salt and water build up inside the cells and, without sufficient moisture, the mucus and fluids that the body produces become thick and sticky.

Gene mutations

A gene mutation is a gene that has changed its structure and so is different from the normal gene. Scientists have found over 1000 different mutations of the CF gene. Some mutations cause milder symptoms than others. Three out of four people with cystic fibrosis are affected by a particular gene mutation, called Delta F508. About one in 25 of the general population carry a copy of the CF gene. These people are known as carriers – they do not have the disease as they have one mutated and one

▲ *We inherit genes from both of our parents.*

normal copy of the gene. In order to have cystic fibrosis you must have a pair of mutated, or faulty, CF genes.

Inheriting the cystic fibrosis gene

If both parents are carriers of a faulty CF gene, there is a one in four chance that their child will inherit two faulty genes – one from each parent – and have cystic fibrosis. There is a two in four chance that their child will inherit only one faulty gene and one normal gene, and be a carrier, and a one in four chance that their child will inherit two normal genes. If only one parent is a carrier, there is a 50 per cent chance that their children will inherit the gene and also be carriers, but they will not be at risk of having the disease.

JAMES FRASER BROWN

In 2006, Gordon Brown, who later became prime minister of the UK, announced that his son James Fraser had been diagnosed with cystic fibrosis. Rosie Barnes of the Cystic Fibrosis Trust said 'I believe [James] Fraser was tested at birth for cystic fibrosis so it would be diagnosed just a few weeks after he was born... If that test takes place, it's very quick and treatment can start immediately... A child diagnosed at birth and treated immediately should remain quite well.'

▼ *This diagram shows the risk of inheriting the CF gene from parents who both carry the faulty gene.*

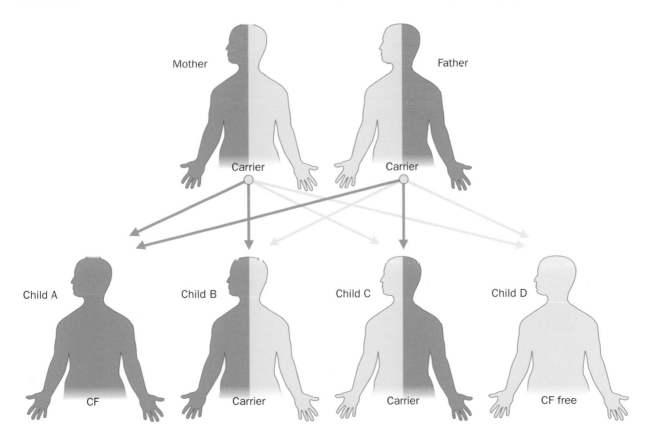

Mother — Carrier

Father — Carrier

Child A — CF

Child B — Carrier

Child C — Carrier

Child D — CF free

Screening and diagnosis

All babies born in the UK are now routinely screened for cystic fibrosis just after birth. Australia, some European countries, and many states in the USA have similar newborn screening programmes.

The Guthrie test

All newborn babies are screened for serious conditions using the Guthrie test. A spot of blood is taken from the baby's heel and tested in a laboratory for abnormalities, including a marker for CF in the blood. Before screening was introduced, babies and children with CF were often not diagnosed until they fell ill. In some cases, parents might have noticed symptoms, such as a baby's salty skin, or felt that something was wrong without knowing why. In others, babies might have shown symptoms, such as chest infections, or diarrhoea and bowel problems, or been very hungry but failed to put on weight.

Genetic testing

Parents who have a family history of cystic fibrosis or who want to know if they are carriers can have a genetic carrier test which identifies up to 90 per cent of cystic fibrosis mutations. A mouthwash or mouth swab is used to take a small sample of saliva which is then genetically tested. A blood sample may also be used for testing. If one or both parents are found to be carriers, they can decide to have a prenatal genetic test on their baby in the womb.

▶ *The Guthrie test can detect over 30 rare but serious health problems including cystic fibrosis.*

Prenatal genetic tests are carried out at around 11 or 12 weeks of pregnancy to check for genetic abnormalities, either by taking a small sample of the placenta or the amniotic fluid that surrounds a baby in the womb. The tests carry a small risk to the baby, so they are usually only carried out

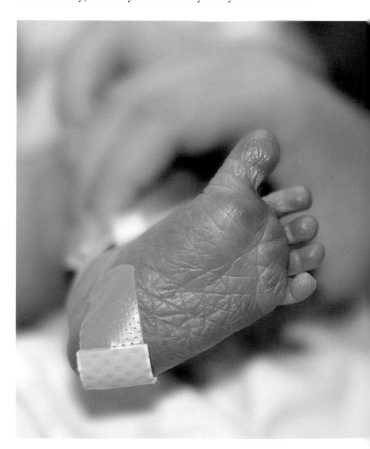

GENETIC SCREENING

An IVF procedure called 'PGD' (pre-implantation genetic diagnosis) can be offered to parents who both carry the faulty CF gene. Doctors create several embryos by fertilising the mother's egg with the father's sperm. The embryos are genetically tested for cystic fibrosis, and only those without the faulty CF gene are implanted into the mother's womb to develop into babies.

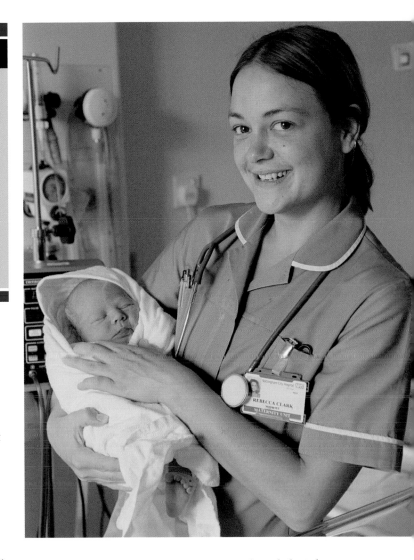

▲ *Midwives can carry out sweat tests soon after a baby is born if there is a chance that he or she has CF.*

when there is a high chance of cystic fibrosis. In the past, mothers have had to wait up to three weeks for the results of prenatal genetic tests. However, a new test called 'Amnio-PCR' takes a sample of amniotic fluid and uses a computer to analyse it. It can produce results with 100 per cent accuracy in around 48 hours. This test is not yet widely available.

Newborn diagnosis

Most people are diagnosed with cystic fibrosis as babies or infants, although some are not diagnosed until later childhood or even adolescence. Early diagnosis means that they can receive treatment before their health worsens. If a screening test shows that there is a high likelihood that a baby has CF, a sweat test is carried out. A small sample of sweat is collected and sent to a laboratory for testing. The test examines the level of salt in the sweat. This is unusually high in people with cystic fibrosis. The CF diagnosis is confirmed by a sweat test.

'*We know early diagnosis in cystic fibrosis is essential to avoid long term damage for lungs and to help patients develop into healthy individuals. This is a life-limiting disease, but the prognosis is improving all the time. The earlier we can intervene and the earlier we start treatment, the better the results will be.*' Dr Felix Ratjen, Hospital for Sick Children, Ontario, Canada

The effects of cystic fibrosis

Cystic fibrosis affects many different organs throughout the body, including the lungs, airways and digestive system. It also affects all the glands in the body that produce mucus and other body fluids.

The lungs

While a normal, thin coating of mucus helps the lungs to clear away germs, the thick mucus created by the CF gene can trap germs, causing frequent infections in the chest (see page 22-23). The mucus can also block the lungs and airways, causing coughing and some breathing difficulties.

The pancreas

The pancreas is an organ in the abdomen, behind the stomach and close to the spine. It produces digestive enzymes which travel through ducts to the intestines. They break down food so the body can absorb essential nutrients. The sticky mucus that is produced in a person with cystic fibrosis can block the ducts and prevent the enzymes from reaching the intestines so that food, especially fats, are not digested properly. This can result in poor nutrition, malabsorption and slow growth in babies and children. Children with CF can also have difficulty gaining and maintaining a healthy body weight.

Bowel problems

When food is not being properly digested and absorbed, there can be problems with bowels and intestines functioning normally. The bowel can fill with large, greasy stools, causing irritation and bloating. The small bowel (or small intestine) can even become blocked, resulting in pain, cramps and constipation.

Diabetes

As well as enzymes, the pancreas also produces insulin, a hormone that helps to control blood glucose levels. Over time in people with cystic fibrosis, the pancreas may begin to be damaged, slowing down or even stopping the production of insulin. This can result in the condition called CF related diabetes, or CFRD, in which the body does not produce enough insulin. This means that it cannot control blood glucose levels, so they can become too high or too low. Teenagers with CF may need to be screened annually for CFRD as symptoms are not always easy to spot.

The liver

The liver acts like a chemical factory in the body. One of its many jobs is to produce bile, a fluid that contains the salts that we need to digest fats from our food. Bile leaves the liver through a network of ducts and is carried to the gall bladder where it becomes more concentrated. The gall bladder then releases it into the small intestine. In cystic fibrosis, these ducts become blocked with sticky mucus, causing the liver to become inflamed. Over time, this can lead to damage and scarring of the liver, known as cirrhosis.

Bone mineral density

Bone health is affected by body weight and lung disease. In people with cystic fibrosis, frequent infections can cause bones to become thin and weak at an earlier age than normal. Some drugs used for cystic fibrosis, such as steroids, may also lower bone strength. The strength of bones is measured by the amount of minerals they contain, and this is known as 'bone mineral density' (BMD). About a third of children with cystic fibrosis have low BMD, which makes their bones more likely to fracture.

▶ *Cystic fibrosis affects the respiratory and digestive organs.*

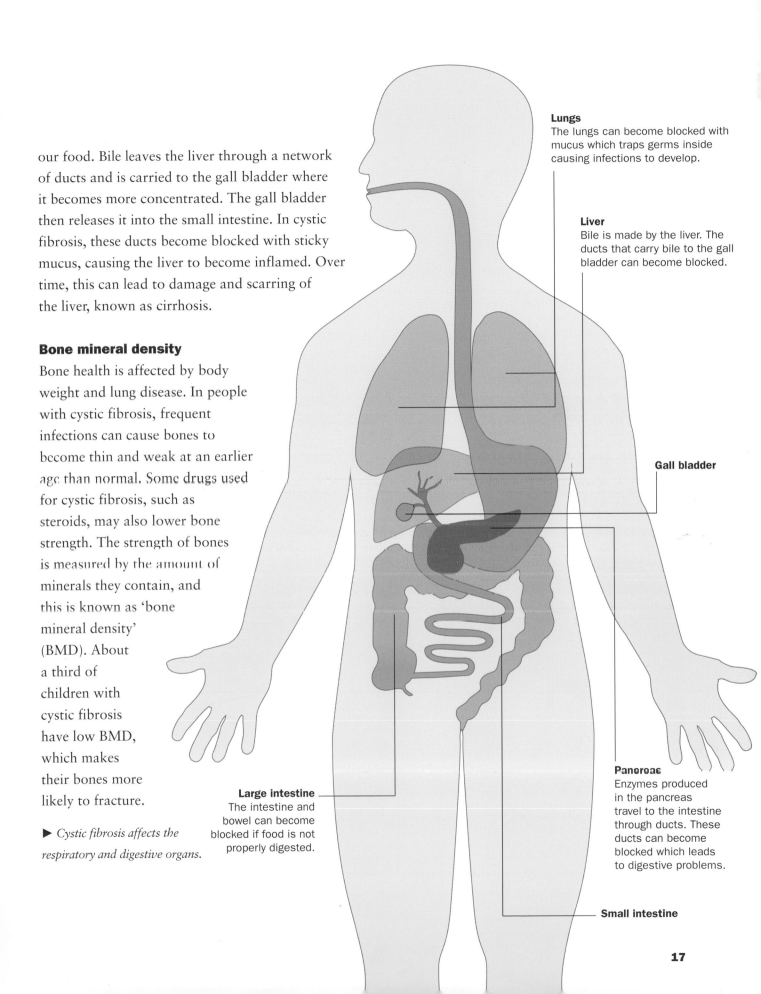

Lungs
The lungs can become blocked with mucus which traps germs inside causing infections to develop.

Liver
Bile is made by the liver. The ducts that carry bile to the gall bladder can become blocked.

Gall bladder

Pancreas
Enzymes produced in the pancreas travel to the intestine through ducts. These ducts can become blocked which leads to digestive problems.

Large intestine
The intestine and bowel can become blocked if food is not properly digested.

Small intestine

How is cystic fibrosis managed?

Cystic fibrosis is a lifelong disorder that needs daily therapy and medication; however most children with cystic fibrosis can live fairly normal and active lives. There are many different aspects to treatment, including medication, diet and chest physiotherapy.

Treatment programmes

Children have regular health checks and tests to monitor their CF and to keep a check on their growth, development and well-being. As all children with cystic fibrosis are affected differently, they each have their own personal treatment programme. Parents and children work alongside CF specialists who manage CF care together as a team.

A combination of medication and chest physiotherapy (see pages 26-27) is needed to maintain nutrition and lung function and prevent chest infections developing. Children are also

▼ *People with CF see their doctor regularly to discuss their health and any changes in medication.*

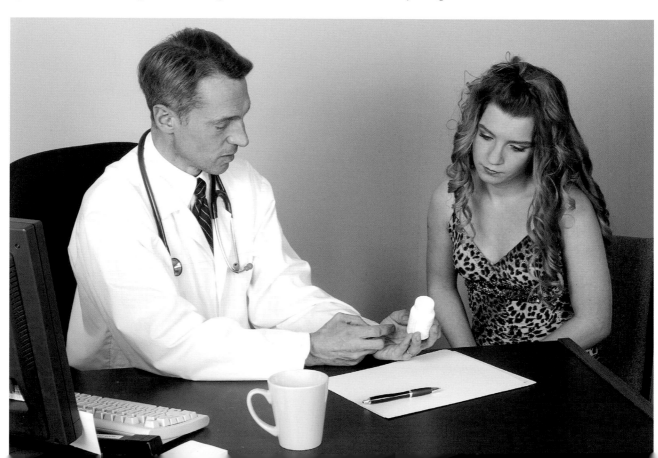

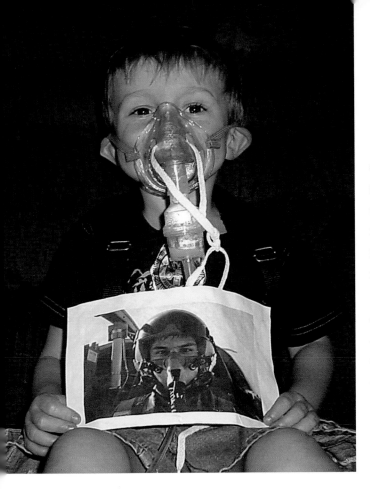

▲ *Games and role play can help young children accept treatment. This little boy imagines he is a fighter pilot when he wears his nebuliser mask (see below).*

encouraged to exercise and take part in sports and active games as this helps lung function and bone and muscle strength.

Medication

Many children with cystic fibrosis use inhalers similar to those used by people with asthma. Some of these help to keep their airways open, especially before exercise. At home, they may use a nebuliser, a portable machine that delivers medicine as a fine mist. They breathe in the mist through a mask or mouthpiece. Nebulisers are used to give antibiotics and other kinds of medication, such as bronchodilators. These medicines open up the airways by relaxing the surrounding muscles, helping to relieve feelings of shortness of breath and chest tightness. Other inhaled medications

called 'mucolytics' help to thin and break down sticky mucus and make it easier to clear and cough up. Most traditional nebulisers are used at home for around 20 minutes twice a day, but electronic nebulisers work much faster and only need about five minutes to deliver medication.

Antibiotics

Most children with cystic fibrosis take antibiotics every day. Antibiotics are used to prevent and control lung infections. If a chest infection develops, the dose may need to be increased, or they may need another type of antibiotic to be given as tablets or intravenously. Intravenous drugs are injected directly into the bloodstream through a tube, usually in a hospital, so they can work faster and more efficiently.

SALT WATER THERAPY

Researchers have found that inhaling a strong saltwater solution can improve lung function and reduce the need for antibiotics in treating cystic fibrosis. Researchers in Australia noted that surfers with cystic fibrosis had fewer than average lung infections. Most of us have a thin layer of water that lines the airways and helps us to clear mucus from our lungs by sweeping it into the mouth where it can be swallowed. In cystic fibrosis, this layer can be dehydrated. Salt water nebulisers use salt to move water out of the lungs, restoring a thin layer of water in the airways. Some people benefit from using a nebuliser to inhale a saltwater solution daily.

The cystic fibrosis team

A team of specialist doctors, nurses, physiotherapists, dieticians and clinical psychologists work together to manage people with CF. Patients see most members of their team during their regular hospital check-ups.

Specialist doctors

Doctors who treat people with CF will usually be specialists in respiratory (chest) medicine. The doctor monitors the weight, height and lung function regularly and also reviews cough swabs or sputum samples to ensure the bacteria that are present in the lungs are treated. Doctors will prescribe any medication and supplements that are needed and can also refer patients to other specialists if they need treatment for other conditions, such as CF related diabetes or pregnancy.

CF clinical nurse specialist

Each person with CF has a specialist nurse who works with families to manage day-to-day treatment. They can also monitor lung function at home, check how people take their medication and manage their nebulisers and physiotherapy. Specialist nurses offer home and school visits when they are needed and can help patients to decide how their routine will be managed. Nurses can also arrange for IV (intravenous) treatments to be continued at home on discharge from hospital. Patients often find it easy to talk to their CF nurse about any worries they have, as they get to know them very well.

▶ *Children with CF see their specialist nurse regularly and often find them easy to talk to about their concerns.*

Physiotherapists

A physiotherapist uses special exercises and physiotherapy regimes to help look after the lungs of patients with CF. Physiotherapists teach parents of children with CF physiotherapy and exercises to help clear the airways of mucus. When children are old enough they are taught to do the physiotherapy themselves. Physiotherapists can help people with

▲ *Patients with CF discuss their health with all the members of their CF team to work out what care is best for them.*

CF to work out how to fit physiotherapy sessions into their daily lives. The physiotherapist will decide which exercises suit each person best and help to design a programme that will suit the person's individual needs.

Dieticians

Dieticians help people with CF to make sure that they are getting enough nutrition from the food that they eat. They give advice on the special diet that people with CF need and how they can include the right high-calorie and fat-rich foods in their diet (see pages 24-25). They advise people with CF on how many enzyme tablets to take before they eat. They also check that a child is getting enough nutrition from school meals and suggest snacks they could take to school with them to boost their calorie intake. Dieticians advise parents about the food their child with CF should eat. With the CF nurse, they suggest ways to explain the child's dietary needs to the school. A dietician also advises patients when the dietary needs vary, for example, during illness or pregnancy, or if the patient has diabetes.

Clinical psychologists

A clinical psychologist is a doctor who specialises in the study of the mind, people's thoughts and their behaviour. They work with people with CF and their families to help them to deal with CF and the effect that it may have on their lives. Initially parents may need some help to accept the fact that their child has been diagnosed with CF, and to understand the impact that this will have. Certain aspects of CF can be difficult for children, teenagers or adults to cope with, and psychologists can provide support and counselling to help people to deal with any stress and anxiety caused by the condition.

Infections and illness

Everyone has chest infections or other illnesses from time to time. When someone has cystic fibrosis, they are more at risk of developing frequent and sometimes serious chest infections.

Chest infections

When infections develop in the lungs, they can lead to inflammation and cause periods of ill health with coughing, wheezing and breathlessness. This can mean frequent visits to cystic fibrosis clinics and hospitals, especially as children get older. If a serious chest infection develops, they may need to be admitted to hospital.

There are thousands of different types of bacteria in the world that can cause infections, but a few affect people with CF more than others. Antibiotics are regularly prescribed, but there is a small risk that some bacteria can become resistant to the antibiotics, making infections difficult to treat. Over time, persistent chest infections have a damaging effect on lung function, and this can mean that as children with cystic fibrosis become adults, they are more likely to face frequent periods of ill health and hospital stays. The body uses its energy resources in fighting chest infections, and illness can cause poor appetite and weight loss. Some people with CF need to have extra feeding (through a tube directly into their stomach) for a time to boost their calorie intake and nutrition.

MOBILE TECHNOLOGY

In some CF centres, mobile phones are being used to help monitor lung function in young people with cystic fibrosis. The phone is attached to a lung function monitor which the patient blows into each day. The readings are sent to hospital computers via the phone. Doctors hope that this data will give warning of infections and worsening lung function, allowing early intervention and treatment, which could help to prevent the need for hospital admission.

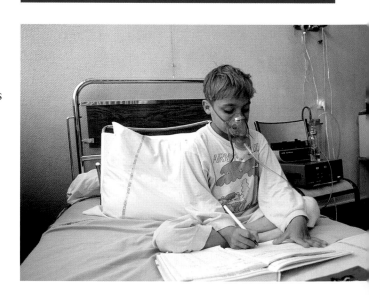

▶ *Serious infections require hospital treatment.*

Cross infection

Many bacteria are harmless to most people, but some can cause an infection in those with cystic fibrosis. Bacteria can be passed on between people by sharing rooms, cutlery or crockery with someone else, or by coughing or kissing. This makes everyday hygiene important to try to avoid cross infection, especially between people with cystic fibrosis if they share medical equipment or do physio together. It is also important to be up to date with immunisations and to have a regular 'flu jab' to prevent the influenza infection during winter.

Smoking

Smoking and passive smoking are known to increase the risk of chest infections and other health complications. Scientists in the USA found that passive smoking (breathing in second-hand smoke) can weaken lung function in people with cystic fibrosis. One specific cystic fibrosis gene mutation doubled the effects of passive smoking, reducing lung function by ten per cent.

GARLIC

Scientists at the University of Nottingham are leading a pilot study to find out whether garlic could help cystic fibrosis patients. They are hoping that garlic capsules may help to prevent a certain bacteria, called pseudomonas, from multiplying and causing infections. Researchers will monitor levels of the bacteria in patients' saliva, as well as their lung function and body weight, during the study.

▲ *Infections spread easily through droplets in the air that can be passed from person to person by coughing and sneezing.*

A special diet

All children need to eat a variety of foods to have a healthy diet, but children with cystic fibrosis need to eat a different diet from other children.

Children with cystic fibrosis need a diet that is high in fats and calories, and therefore energy. This is because their pancreas is not able to release the enzymes that their body needs in order to digest foods properly, so nutrients may not be properly absorbed. Children with cystic fibrosis need extra calories to grow and develop properly, and to help them to get enough energy from their food. A healthy body weight helps them to fight chest infections, and gives them reserves to draw on if they become ill and lose weight.

Which foods?

In order for children with CF to grow and maintain body weight, they need to eat more fatty and high-energy foods than are normally recommended for a healthy diet. Foods that contain protein and fats, such as meat, dairy foods, oily fish and nuts are a good source of energy. Sugary foods like biscuits, chocolate and puddings are also high in calories. These foods should be balanced with carbohydrates, such as bread, potatoes or pasta, other protein foods, including non-oily fish and eggs, and plenty of foods that provide fibre and vitamins, such as fresh fruit and vegetables.

Enzyme and vitamin supplements

When we eat, our bodies absorb nutrients from our food, including vitamins, fats and proteins. As children with cystic fibrosis are often unable to absorb nutrients properly, vitamin supplements may be needed. Most children with CF also take enzyme tablets with meals and snacks which

◀ *High-fat foods – which should be limited in normal diets – are needed to boost weight gain and energy levels.*

DIET AND ENZYMES

Melissa is 13 years old. She first began to show symptoms of cystic fibrosis when she was eight. Melissa needs to take 30 enzyme tablets every day. If she doesn't, she becomes really uncomfortable and bloated, and suffers from diarrhoea. Because it is hard for Melissa's body to get enough fat from the food she eats, her mum often cooks food in a way that will add fat to her diet, such as frying or roasting rather than grilling or baking. She makes sure Melissa has plenty of foods that contain fats and protein, including oily fish, nuts, dairy foods and meat, and always uses full fat dairy products in meals. Melissa says; 'I have to remember to take my enzyme tablets with every meal or even if I am just having a snack. I also have to see my dietician regularly to check that I am getting enough nutrients from my food. Sometimes she tells me I need a supplement. It's most likely when I've got a chest infection because that means I don't have much appetite so I can be short of particular nutrients or vitamins. I usually take the supplement in fruit juice or a milkshake.'

help them to absorb fats and proteins. Doctors or dieticians advise on the type and amount of enzyme tablets that should be taken, and this is generally calculated alongside the fat content of meals, snacks and drinks.

Clearing the airways

Every day, children and adults with cystic fibrosis need to clear their airways of mucus. If mucus is allowed to build up, it can stop the lungs from working properly and increase the risk of serious chest infections. There are several different physiotherapy techniques that can be used, known as airway clearance techniques (ACTs). These are practised alongside regular exercise.

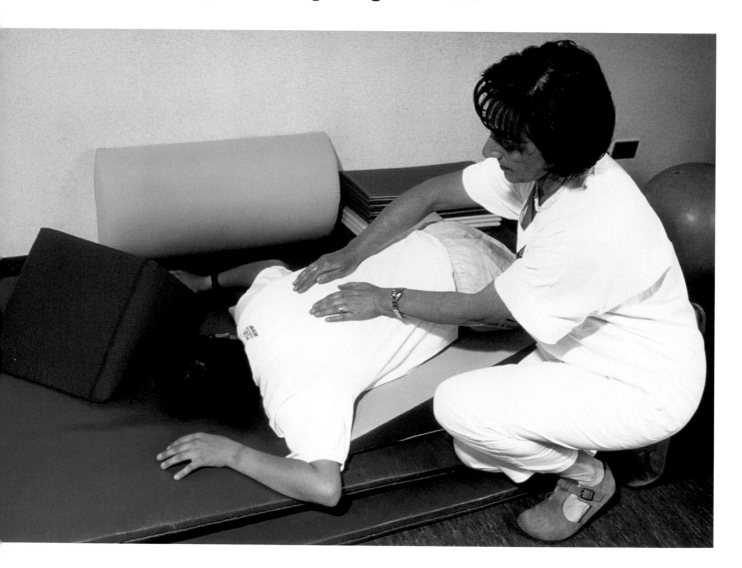

Chest physiotherapy

Most children with cystic fibrosis have chest physiotherapy twice a day. This is sometimes called 'postural drainage and percussion'. Parents are taught the technique by physiotherapists at a cystic fibrosis clinic. The child sits or lies down with their head supported while the parent or carer pats and pummels their back, chest and sides to loosen mucus so the child can cough it up. Physiotherapy needs to be done either before or a couple of hours after meals. The amount of time spent on physio depends on each child and can last anywhere from 15 to 30 minutes. Some children may only need one treatment a day, but others may need up to four treatments a day when the mucus is bad (especially if they have an infection). From around the age of nine, children may start learning to do their own physiotherapy treatments.

Breathing aids

Physiotherapists teach children breathing exercises which can help them to breathe out more fully and strengthen the muscles used for breathing. For young children, these can be taught as blowing, breathing and counting games. 'Directed coughing' is another technique that teaches a pattern of breathing and coughing which helps to loosen mucus. Children take a deep breath, then hold their breath before 'huffing' and forcing air out of their lungs, using their hands and arms to help them.

◀ *Physiotherapists give treatment and teach techniques to children and their families.*

CASE NOTES

LISA'S STORY

Twelve-year-old Lisa has her first chest physiotherapy of the day before breakfast. It helps to clear all the sticky mucus that builds up in her lungs overnight. Lisa lies on the sofa and turns over halfway through to make sure that all the mucus is cleared. Most days, she has physiotherapy for around 20 minutes in the morning and a longer session of up to 45 minutes in the evening. When the mucus is bad, she might have it more frequently, up to four times a day. 'I am so used to the routine, I don't mind physio and it doesn't hurt me,' Lisa explains. 'The worst thing is it can be boring having to spend up to an hour doing physio, and it is something that we have to fit into the day whatever else is going on. Mostly I listen to music which helps pass the time.' Lisa's mum has told her that as she is growing up, she must learn to do her physiotherapy herself.

Some children also use special physiotherapy vests that fill with air and then vibrate, forcing air in to and out of the lungs to loosen the mucus. They can then cough to clear the mucus. Children as young as two or three can use these vests, and different sizes are made so that parents can replace them as the child grows.

Some children prefer to use hand-held devices that they blow into. There are different types, such as a flutter valve which has a steel ball inside that vibrates into their lungs when they blow into it, or an acapella, which has a magnetic force inside that helps to loosen mucus from the lungs.

Physical exercise

Exercise is essential alongside physiotherapy and can help people with cystic fibrosis to stay fit and healthy. Children with cystic fibrosis are encouraged to take part in sports and games both in and out of school. Exercise can improve physical health, muscle and bone strength, as well as general well-being.

Exercise programmes

Physiotherapists can help children and adults with cystic fibrosis to plan an exercise programme to suit their needs. They work alongside dieticians to make sure that children have a healthy diet so that exercise does not increase weight loss, but helps them to build up and tone body muscle. During any kind of exercise, people with cystic fibrosis should drink plenty of fluids to avoid dehydration. In hot weather, salt tablets or isotonic sports drinks may also help replace the salt lost through sweating. If a child has cystic fibrosis related diabetes (see page 16), exercise can help control blood glucose levels and reduce the need for insulin. However, food intake must be carefully managed to make sure that blood glucose levels do not fall too low.

▼ *Exercise helps children with cystic fibrosis develop strength and stamina.*

Cardiovascular exercise

It is important that people with cystic fibrosis take part in cardiovascular exercise, such as running, cycling or swimming. During cardiovascular exercise the muscles in the body need more oxygen to work. This makes the lungs and heart work harder to deliver oxygen. This in turn makes the heart stronger and keeps blood pressure at a healthy level, improving general fitness. A fit body is generally more able to fight off infections, which can mean fewer and shorter hospital stays for people with cystic fibrosis.

Cardiovascular exercise creates a natural vibration in the lungs that helps to loosen mucus, making it easier to cough up. Exercise can also stimulate coughing, helping to clear the lungs, build stamina and reduce breathlessness. Stretching exercises can also help by maintaining flexibility in the joints and muscles around the shoulders and chest. Younger children can take part in games and sports, such as wheelbarrow racing and trampolining, to keep the upper body flexible and help breathing. Some children with cystic fibrosis may need to use an inhaler to open the airways before doing physical activity (see page 19).

Weight-bearing exercise

Weight-bearing exercises, using hand held weights or resistance machines in a gym can increase bone mineral density (see page 17) which strengthens bones. They can also help to increase physical strength and bulk, which can improve body image and increase self-esteem.

▶ *Developing skills in team sports improves self-esteem as well as physical health.*

MATTY'S STORY

Matty is 13 years old and was diagnosed with cystic fibrosis shortly before his second birthday. Matty has been a keen swimmer since the age of seven. He trains five times a week and regularly competes for the Middlesbrough Amateur Swimming Club. He recently competed in the 1,500 metres front crawl. Matty has been given a Breathing Life Award from the Cystic Fibrosis Trust and was named Junior Sports Person of the Year at a national awards ceremony. When he is not swimming, Matty also enjoys cross-country running and playing football. Last year he got together with fellow swimmers Adam Jones, 14, and Sarah Gibbon, 13, to complete the Junior Great North Run for charity. Together they collected more than £650 for research into cystic fibrosis.

Cystic fibrosis and families

When a child with cystic fibrosis is born, family life and routines have to change and adapt. There are prescriptions to collect, regular treatments to fit into the day and frequent visits to cystic fibrosis clinics and hospitals for health checks or treatments.

Food and hygiene

Children with cystic fibrosis may need to have a different diet from other family members (see pages 24-25). They may also need to use separate cutlery or crockery if anyone in the family has a cold, flu or other virus, to avoid catching germs that could lead to a serious chest infection.

Everyday hygiene, such as careful hand washing, is especially important when a member of the family falls ill.

▼ *Using nebulisers and other daily therapies must be fitted into normal family life.*

Parents and siblings

It is normal for parents to worry about the health and future of their child with cystic fibrosis. When parents discover that they both carry the faulty CF gene, they often seek medical advice if they are considering having more children. Cystic fibrosis will also have an impact on siblings. It can be worrying and unsettling for them when a brother or sister falls ill and has to go into hospital. Parents also need to spend extra time with a child with cystic fibrosis, for example when giving chest physiotherapy, washing out nebulisers and preparing medication.

Sometimes siblings can feel left out if their brother or sister is taking up a lot of their parents' attention. It can help if they get involved in everyday treatments. For example, older siblings might learn to do chest physiotherapy for a brother or sister with cystic fibrosis.

Planning

Families find different ways to remember all the medication and treatments that need to be given each day to a person with cystic fibrosis. Some use text message reminders, wall calendars or spreadsheets on a computer. When families plan holidays, or even days out, they have to consider how to manage routine treatments, such as using nebulisers and having chest physiotherapy. It can be difficult to make spontaneous plans because there is always medication to be packed up, and set times for treatments to be considered. All families are supported by their CF teams to ensure that CF fits into their family life.

CASE NOTES

JORDAN'S STORY

Jordan is 14. He enjoys swimming, football and playing games on his computer. Jordan was diagnosed with cystic fibrosis when he was just a few weeks old. He has to take enzymes and antibiotics and have two sessions of chest physiotherapy every day. When he has taken his medication he puts a tick on a special chart that records what he has taken and when. Jordan's mum recently moved house which meant Jordan could have a room of his own. Before that, he shared with his younger brother Luke, which meant that when Luke had coughs or colds, Jordan was more at risk of catching them. When he was nine, Jordan had his first serious lung infection. 'The doctors told me I would have to start using a nebuliser for my antibiotic treatment,' Jordan recalls. 'Because this [infection] kept coming back, I have to use the nebuliser every day. Normally I use it twice a day, before I go to school and in the evening. Mum says we might be able to get one of the new e-flow nebulisers soon and that would be great because they take less than five minutes, which would mean I have more time for other things like football!'

Cystic fibrosis at school

Many children with cystic fibrosis live full and active school lives, but teachers and classroom helpers should be aware of the child's condition so they are able to give appropriate support. CF nurses visit schools to teach the staff about the condition.

'I can do everything that my friends do. I do quite a lot of after-school activities. I do ballet and swimming. I enjoy cycling and I do drama. I can join in with PE at school. The doctors really encourage me to do exercise.'
Jessica, aged 12

In the classroom

Persistent coughing can be embarrassing for a child, especially when a coughing attack produces mucus or makes the child sick. Teachers should be aware that children may need to be excused from class more often than usual if they have digestive problems and need to go to the toilet frequently. Some children may encounter bullying because they are small or underweight for their age, or be teased for taking enzyme tablets with their lunch. It helps if friends can support the child and be involved in helping with physiotherapy and other treatment routines. Children with CF often have a best friend who knows a lot about them and can offer support.

Daily treatments

Routine treatments, such as chest physiotherapy or using a nebuliser, must be fitted into the school day and they can mean children have less time than others for coursework or homework. Teachers or school nurses generally provide support, but in a few cases a parent or other carer may need to come into school to help with treatments.

Illness and absence

When a child has cystic fibrosis, their health can vary from month to month, or even day to day. Although sports and physical activity are an important part of keeping well for children with

▼ *Children with cystic fibrosis often need to be excused from lessons to go to the toilet or to cough outside.*

cystic fibrosis, there can be times when their energy levels are low. Colds or chest infections can leave children feeling unusually tired. They can also lead to frequent absences from school. A serious chest infection may mean a long absence from school, especially if a child needs hospital treatment. Teachers may be able to set work to be done at home if the child is well enough. Older children can sometimes use portable IV devices, which are like small pumps, to give antibiotics under supervision at home or at school.

Exams

Some children with cystic fibrosis are placed on special needs registers so they can qualify for special arrangements regarding their health needs, for example in exams. Exam boards can make concessions for children with cystic fibrosis, for example, by allowing exams to be taken at home,

▲ *Friends can provide valuable support once they know and understand the issues involved with having cystic fibrosis.*

or by giving permission for supervised breaks for treatments or allowing extra time for an exam. Good communication between teachers, the CF team and the child and their family will ensure that children get the support they need.

Delayed puberty

For some people with CF, being behind their peers in terms of their growth and development, in particular a delayed onset of puberty, can make them self-conscious and anxious. For boys, cystic fibrosis almost always results in problems with fertility. Schools need to be sensitive in the way they provide sex education and some teenagers may need counselling to help overcome their worries.

Growing up with cystic fibrosis

As children get older, they learn to balance their daily treatments with their education, as well as their social lives and relationships. Daily therapies can take one to two hours or more a day even when they are well. If they fall ill, they may need to go into hospital for treatment.

Transition to adult CF centres

Most children move from paediatric cystic fibrosis centres to adult cystic fibrosis centres when they are aged between 16 and 18 years. This means that they begin to take responsibility for their own therapies and medication. This is a planned move, and discussions about adult CF care start during the early secondary school years.

Living away from home

When young people with cystic fibrosis grow up and go to college or university, or leave home, they have to become more independent, caring for themselves and taking full responsibility for their daily routines. This includes remembering to order and collect prescriptions, washing and preparing nebulisers, keeping track of their intake of enzyme and antibiotic tablets, and doing daily chest physiotherapy. Some teenagers find it challenging to adjust, and some may start to neglect their treatments. Mood swings can make them rebel against the demands of their daily routine. It can be hard to balance a normal social life with CF treatments, for example, accepting a spontaneous invitation from a

▲ *Young people with CF have to fit their social lives around daily routines and therapies.*

friend may mean missing a chest physiotherapy session, or not taking the enzymes needed to digest food properly.

Higher education

Young people going to university or college need to consider where the nearest cystic fibrosis centre is, and whether there is an on-campus pharmacy or medical centre. They will need to make sure that the pharmacy keeps their essential medication in stock, such as enzymes and antibiotics. They also have to think about the type of course that will suit them best. Modular courses are more flexible as they offer the chance of re-taking modules if they are missed because of illness. Some young people may find that their health is worse when they try to do too much, or are under stress, such as during exam times. It is important they take care of their health by avoiding contact with people who have colds or viruses and making sure they take vitamin supplements and get a flu jab as soon as it is offered.

Travel

When people with cystic fibrosis travel, they must remember to pack all the medication and equipment needed to continue therapies away from home. Keeping equipment clean and following recommended diets and treatments can be hard when travelling overseas, but can be done with planning and preparation. There is lots of information about international travel with CF on the internet.

▼ *It can be challenging keeping up with treatments and medication when travelling on backpacking or adventure holidays.*

New treatments

Improvements in treatment have meant that many more people with cystic fibrosis are living well into adulthood. There are already more adults than children living with cystic fibrosis. There are many on-going studies and clinical trials to find new treatments for some of the symptoms of cystic fibrosis.

Diet and nutrition

Some scientists are developing therapies based on diet and nutrition. Normal lungs appear to have more natural antioxidants than lungs affected by cystic fibrosis. Antioxidants are found in fresh fruit and vegetables and boost the body's immune system. Scientists believe that people with cystic fibrosis may not be absorbing them sufficiently. They suggest that antioxidants could be used to slow down, or even prevent, lung disease in people with cystic fibrosis. They are looking at ways of boosting antioxidant intake through the development of vitamin supplements that can be more easily absorbed by the body.

Fatty acids

Another area of research is concentrating on fatty acids. These are found naturally in the body and also in certain foods, such as oily fish and nuts. Scientists believe that an imbalance of fatty acids may cause lung inflammation. Research studies in the USA have found that raised levels of certain fatty acids and lower levels of others may make the lungs more likely to become inflamed. They are looking at ways of correcting the imbalance through the use of supplements, such as Omega 3 fish oils.

Drugs

Scientists are also developing new drugs to treat cystic fibrosis in different parts of the body. Some intravenous antibiotics that are currently used need long-term courses and can cause side effects, including headaches and hearing problems. Scientists are developing antibiotics that need less frequent doses and may have fewer side effects. New drugs are also being tested, which aim to correct the abnormal salt and water balance in cells.

CHEMICAL CAUSES

New research studies have found lower than normal levels of two chemicals in the mucus of patients with cystic fibrosis. Some scientists believe that this means that less mucus than normal is being produced in the airways, and the lungs are being blocked not by mucus, but by damaged lung cells and bacteria. This is a new theory, which is challenging many of the established beliefs about cystic fibrosis.

Transcripts

Some people with CF may find that their lung function falls so they have difficulty walking, breathing and managing daily life. If so, they may be assessed for a lung transplant. If accepted, they are often placed on a waiting list. Although a lung transplant is a major operation that requires four to six weeks in hospital and several months of recovery, it can offer people with CF a better quality of life. After a transplant, patients need to go on taking medication and monitor their lung function every day using a spirometer, which measures the amount of air going in and out of the lungs. About one in twelve people with cystic fibrosis may need a liver transplant if their liver becomes damaged (see pages 16-17).

'The transplant I had was literally life changing. I have now graduated from college, found a new, active social life and am working in the club and fashion industry, specialising in photography. Hopefully a long, successful career awaits. Without the transplant none of this would have been possible. It allows a life without the restraints of CF – although it isn't a cure, it can feel very much like it!'
Joe, aged 19

▼ *Joe had a heart and lung transplant four years ago; since then he has been living life to the full.*

The future

Scientists hope that one day they will be able to find a cure for cystic fibrosis. They are constantly developing new ideas for ways in which symptoms can be relieved, or cured.

Gene therapy

Scientists hope to be able to correct the faulty CF gene by adding normal copies of it to cells in the lungs. The key problem is how to get the cells lining the lungs to accept the new gene. The difficulty is that the lungs are organs designed to keep out 'invaders'. They have defences in place so that inhaled bacteria and pollutants are removed, but unfortunately these defences also remove the new genes. To overcome this problem, the genes are packaged with 'gene transfer agents'. These include putting the gene into a cold virus, or wrapping the gene in fat globules (liposomes). Whichever method is used, the new gene will only work for a few weeks and so the process needs to be repeated.

Unfortunately, to date it has not been possible to use the cold virus repeatedly as a gene transfer agent because the body's immune system recognises the virus and destroys it. Therefore, most of the work that is going on at present is focused on the use of liposomes to transfer the new gene into the lung cells. Using this system, a large trial has just started in the UK, run by the UK CF Gene Therapy

▼ *A doctor works on research which, it is hoped, will help people with cystic fibrosis.*

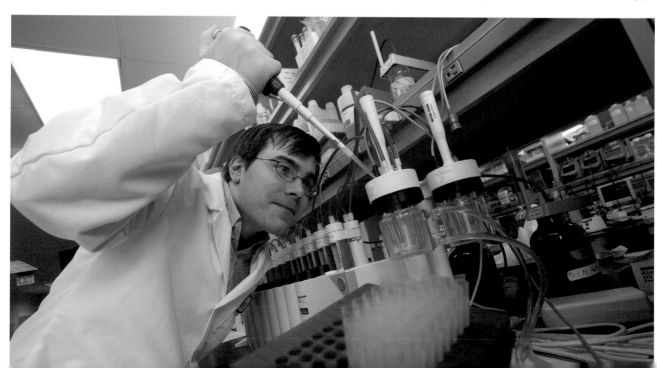

BREATHING LIFE AWARDS

The Cystic Fibrosis Trust holds an annual awards ceremony to celebrate the achievements of those living with cystic fibrosis. The Breathing Life Awards are open to anyone over the age of five who has cystic fibrosis. Awards are given for achievements in the arts and in sport, and also for 'fighting spirit'. They are awarded during a special gala evening of entertainment which is broadcast on television.

▶ *Sportsmen David Seaman (left) and Michael Vaughn (right) with 10-year-old James Holford, who received the Breathing Life Award (see above) for Junior Sport under 11.*

Consortium, to see whether giving the gene repeatedly for one year will improve the lungs of patients with CF.

'The key issue is that we are working against evolution. We're trying to get it into lung cells and lung cells are made to keep things out, … and that's why gene therapy's so difficult because you're trying to put in a new gene into a cell that says no thanks.' Professor Eric Alton, UK Cystic Fibrosis Gene Therapy Consortium, Royal Brompton Hospital, London

Protein repair therapy

Another new approach to treating cystic fibrosis is 'protein repair therapy'. This focuses on repairing the faulty protein that is produced by the CF gene. Scientists hope to be able to correct the way it works to allow salt and water to move more easily around the cells that line the lungs.

Charities

Charities, including the Cystic Fibrosis Trust in the UK and the Cystic Fibrosis Foundation in the USA, are dedicated to funding research into cystic fibrosis, and providing support and information for people with cystic fibrosis and their families. Many young people with cystic fibrosis take part in research studies, which could dramatically improve the quality and length of their lives, and may hopefully lead to a cure in the future.

Glossary

abdomen the part of your body between your chest and your hips

abnormality a problem or feature that is not normally present

acapella a breathing device used for physiotherapy

amniotic fluid the fluid that surrounds an unborn baby in the womb

antibiotic a drug used to fight infections caused by bacteria

antioxidants substances found in fresh fruit and vegetables that may protect the body's cells against damage, and help to prevent infections

asthma a condition that causes breathing problems

bacteria tiny living things that exist everywhere. Some types can be helpful but some can be harmful to the body

bile a fluid which aids digestion that is made in the liver and stored in the gall bladder

bronchodilator a drug that helps to open the airways

cardiovascular exercise exercise that affects the heart and blood vessels by raising the heart rate

calorie a measurement of the amount of energy food is going to give you

carrier someone who has one copy of a gene

chromosomes a tiny strand of genes, made up of DNA, found in each cell

cirrhosis damage or scarring to the liver

clinical psychologist someone who is interested in the mind. They analyse people's thoughts and behaviour

concentrate to make a liquid stronger

constipation when it becomes hard to go to the toilet because the bowel contents are too solid

dehydration not having enough water in your body

diabetes a disorder caused by the pancreas not producing enough insulin, so the level of glucose in the blood is not controlled

diagnose to identify a disease or condition after careful examination of the body and symptoms

dietician someone who advises people about what to eat, especially if they have a condition where a special diet is needed

ducts vessels or channels that carry fluids in the body

embryo an unborn baby that is still developing

enzyme a chemical that controls the speed of chemical reactions in the body

fibre a bulky substance in food that helps food pass through the digestive system

gene the basic unit of heredity by which characteristics are passed from one generation to the next

gene transfer agents a substance that a gene can be put into that will carry the gene into the body

glucose a type of sugar that is found in certain foods and is turned into energy inside the body

immune system the body's natural defence against diseases

immunisation an injection with a vaccine to protect against diseases

infertility inability to have children

inflammation swelling

inhaler a handheld device used to inhale medicines

inherited passed down from parent to child

insulin the hormone produced by the pancreas that helps the body to convert glucose into energy

intravenously to put something into the body through a vein

IVF (in vitro fertilisation) a technique in which egg cells are fertilised outside the womb

laxative a medicine to loosen the bowels

malabsorption when nutrients from food are poorly absorbed into the body through the small intestine

mutation a change in a gene

mucolytics medication that helps to thin and break down mucus

mucus sticky secretions from the mucus membranes in the gut, nose, airways and lungs

nebuliser a portable device for inhaling medicine

nutrients substances that are necessary for growth and health

nutrition the body's way of using food for growth, repair and well-being.

pancreas a gland that produces hormones that help the body to digest food

physiotherapist someone who uses special exercises and forms of massage to treat medical conditions

placenta the organ in the womb that allows substances to pass between the mother's blood and the unborn baby's blood

prenatal before birth

respiratory to do with the process of breathing

side effects the effects that a drug or treatment might have in addition to the desired effects it has. Side effects may be harmful and undesirable

sputum mucus that is coughed up from the lungs in people with cystic fibrosis

stamina strength, power to keep going

swab a sample that can be taken

symptoms changes in the body that indicate that a disease or other condition is present

vitamins substances found in foods that we need for the body to stay healthy

Further information

Books

Cystic Fibrosis (Diseases and Disorders),
Melissa Abramovitz, *Lucent Books 2003*

Cystic Fibrosis: (Genetic Diseases and Disorders),
Maxine Rosaler, *Rosen Publishing Group 2007*

Cystic Fibrosis (Health Watch),
Susan Dudley Gold, *Enslow Publishers 2000*

Cystic Fibrosis: (Perspectives on Diseases and Disorders), Judy Monroe, *Greenhaven Press 2008*

Everything You Need To Know About Cystic Fibrosis (Need to Know Library),
Justin Lee, *Rosen Publishing Group 2001*

Living with Cystic Fibrosis: (Living well: Chronic Conditions), Susan Heinrichs Gray, *Child's World 2003*

Films

A Boy called Alex
A Cutting Edge documentary for Channel 4 about Alex Stobbs, a musical prodigy who has cystic fibrosis. Video clips are available on the Channel 4 website www.channel4.com and on www.youtube.com.

Websites

www.childrenfirst.nhs.uk
A health site for young people on health matters including cystic fibrosis, with advice from experts in child health.

www.cff.org
The website for the Cystic Fibrosis Foundation, the leading CF organisation in the USA, contains lots of information about cystic fibrosis, including first person experiences and stories.

www.cfireland.ie
The website of the Cystic Fibrosis Association of Ireland. They have lots of information about fundraising, publications, research and their Annual Conference. They also have a photo gallery and forum, and links to other cystic fibrosis organisations.

www.cftrust.org.uk
The website of the Cystic Fibrosis Trust, the leading national charity in the UK, which funds research into cystic fibrosis. Information is provided for families, schools and teachers, as well as factsheets and an 'ask the expert' email service.

www.cysticfibrosis.ca
Website of the Canadian Cystic Fibrosis Foundation whose main aim is to fund research into cystic fibrosis and care for those who have it. Their website is packed with information about cystic fibrosis and about the foundation.

www.cysticfibrosis.com
This website has lots of current information on what is going on in the CF community. It hosts discussion groups and forums, has blogs, recent articles and advice about CF.

www.cysticfibrosis.org.au
The Cystic Fibrosis Australia website has lots of information about CF, upcoming events, stories, current research and a forum. They also have links to state organisations.

www.cysticfibrosismedicine.com
A website that provides information on cystic fibrosis, with a chatroom, links and gallery.

www.kidshealth.org/kid/health_problems/heart/cystic_fibrosis.html
An easy to understand introduction to cystic fibrosis and the problems it causes from the Kids' Health website.

www.pwcf.net
A website set up by people with cystic fibrosis with profiles, articles, tips and a chat forum.

www.sibs.org.uk
A website for young people who are growing up with a brother or sister affected by a chronic illness or disability.

Index

These are the list of contents for each title in Explaining:

Asthma
What is asthma? • History of asthma • Increase in asthma • Who has asthma? • Healthy lungs • How asthma affects the lungs • What triggers asthma? • Asthma and allergies • Diagnosing asthma • Preventing an attack • Relieving an attack • What to do during an attack • Growing up with asthma • Living with asthma • Asthma and exercise • Future

Autism
What is autism? • Autism: a brief history • The rise of autism • The autistic spectrum • The signs of autism • Autism and inheritance • The triggers of autism • Autism and the body • Autism and mental health • Can autism be treated? • Living with autism • Autism and families • Autism and school • Asperger syndrome • Autism and adulthood • The future for autism

Blindness
What is blindness? • Causes and effects • Visual impairment • Colour blindness and night blindness • Eye tests • Treatments and cures • Coping with blindness • Optical aids • Guide dogs and canes • Home life • On the move • Blindness and families • Blindness at school • Blindness as an adult • Blindness, sport and leisure • The future for blindness

Cerebral Palsy
What is cerebral palsy? • The causes of cerebral palsy • Diagnosis • Types of cerebral palsy • Other effects of cerebral palsy • Managing cerebral palsy • Other support • Technological support • Communication • How it feels • Everyday life • Being at school • Cerebral palsy and the family • Into adulthood • Raising awareness • The future

Cystic Fibrosis
What is cystic fibrosis? • A brief history • What causes cystic fibrosis? • Screening and diagnosis • The effects of cystic fibrosis • How is cystic fibrosis managed? • Infections and illness • A special diet • Clearing the airways • Physical exercise • Cystic fibrosis and families • Cystic fibrosis at school • Living with cystic fibrosis • Living longer • New treatments • Gene therapy

Deafness
What is deafness? • Ears and sounds • Types of deafness • Causes of deafness • Signs of deafness • Diagnosis • Treating deafness • Lip reading • Sign language • Deafness and education • Schools for the deaf • Deafness and adulthood • Technology • Deafness and the family • Fighting discrimination • Latest research

Diabetes
What is diabetes? • Type 1 diabetes • Type 2 diabetes • Symptoms and diagnosis • Medication • Hypoglycaemia • Eyes, skin and feet • Other health issues • Healthy eating and drinking • Physical activity • Living with diabetes • Diabetes and families • Diabetes at school • Growing up with diabetes • The future for diabetics

Down's syndrome
What is Down's syndrome? • Changing attitudes • Who has Down's Syndrome? • What are chromosomes? • The extra chromosome • Individual differences • Health problems • Testing for Down's Syndrome • Diagnosing at birth • Babies • Toddlers • At school • Friendships and fun • Effects on the family • Living independently • Down's syndrome community

Epilepsy
What is epilepsy? • Causes and effects • Who has epilepsy? • Partial seizures • Generalised seizures • Triggers • Diagnosis • How you can help • Controlling epilepsy • Taking medicines • Living with epilepsy • Epilepsy and families • Epilepsy at school • Sport and leisure • Growing up with epilepsy • The future for epilepsy

Food allergy
What are food allergies? • Food allergies: a brief history • Food aversion, intolerance or allergy? • What is an allergic reaction? • Food allergies: common culprits • Anaphylaxis • Testing for food allergies • Avoiding allergic reactions • Treating allergic reactions • Food allergies on the rise • Food allergies and families • Food allergies and age • Living with food allergies • 21st century problems • The future for food allergies